NUMBER AND ALGEBRA

CODE CRACKER

Lucia found a treasure map. It was written in code.
It said the buried treasure was under a 20 18 5 5.

Where was the treasure buried?

Extension

Make up more treasure map clues like this one.
See if a classmate can work them out.

Strategy hints!

1. Look for the important words in the question.
2. Look for a pattern.

ISBN 978 1 4202 9393 7

LETTERS AND NUMBERS

In a secret code, letters stand for numbers.
In this code, the word BEE is worth 12 points.
The word DOG is worth 26 points.

a) How many points is the word CAT worth?
b) How many points is the word ANT worth?
c) How many points is the word FROG worth?

Extension

Make up a code like this one. Then, write more problems using the code.
See if a classmate can work them out.

Strategy hints!

1 Look for the important words in the question.
2 Look for a pattern.
9 Think logically.

ISBN 978 1 4202 9393 7

FUNNY PATTERN

Z, X, V, T, __, __, N, __

Fill in the 3 gaps in the pattern.

Extension

There are 13 letters in this pattern.

What letters come in 11th, 12th and 13th places?

Strategy hints!

1 Look for the important words in the question.

2 Look for a pattern.

9 Think logically.

ISBN 978 1 4202 9393 7

SYMBOL SHIFTER

In this code, the symbol [*] stands for something.

2 [*] 3 = 6

4 [*] 3 = 8

5 [*] 4 = 10

a) What is 6 [*] 7?

b) What does the symbol [*] stand for?

Extension

Make up a symbol problem like this one.

See if a classmate can work it out.

Strategy hints!

1 Look for the important words in the question.

2 Look for a pattern.

9 Think logically.

ISBN 978 1 4202 9393 7

FIND THE SYMBOL

In this code, the symbol $\boxed{*}$ stands for something.

$10 \boxed{*} 3 = 5$

$8 \boxed{*} 1 = 5$

$6 \boxed{*} 2 = 2$

a) What is $9 \boxed{*} 2$?

b) What does the symbol $\boxed{*}$ stand for?

Extension

Make up some more problems like this one.
See if a classmate can work them out.

Strategy hints!

1. Look for the important words in the question.
2. Look for a pattern.
9. Think logically.

ISBN 978 1 4202 9393 7

CRAZY CALCULATOR

Professor Digit types 10 into his calculator and sees 1 come onto the screen.
He then types 23 and sees 5 come onto the screen.
He then types 26.

What will come onto his screen?

Extension

Make up a crazy calculator problem like this one.
See if a classmate can work it out.

Strategy hints!

1 Look for the important words in the question.
2 Look for a pattern.
9 Think logically.

ISBN 978 1 4202 9393 7

DIZZY DIGITS

Professor Digit types 51 into his calculator and sees 4 come onto the screen.
He then types 30 and sees 3 come onto the screen.
He then types 74.

What will come onto his screen?

Strategy hints!

1. Look for the important words in the question.
2. Look for a pattern.
9. Think logically.

Extension

Make up a crazy calculator problem like this one.
See if a classmate can work it out.

ISBN 978 1 4202 9393 7

BOXED IN

Fill in the boxes by using the numbers 3, 6 and 2 to make the number sentence true.

$$4 + \square - \square + \square = 9$$

Find out if there is more than one answer to the problem.

Extension

Fill in the boxes by using the numbers 7, 4 and 3 to make the number sentence true.

$$5 + \square - \square - \square = 5$$

Find out if there is more than one answer to the problem.

Strategy hints!

1 Look for the important words in the question.

9 Think logically.

ISBN 978 1 4202 9393 7

INSIDE THE BOX

Fill in the boxes by using the numbers 4, 5, 10 and 1 to make the number sentence true.

$\square - \square - \square = 2 - \square$

Find out if there is more than one answer to the problem.

Extension

Fill in the boxes by using the numbers 3, 10, 11 and 12 to make the number sentence true.

$\square + \square - \square = 14 - \square$

Find out if there is more than one answer to the problem.

Strategy hints!

1 Look for the important words in the question.

9 Think logically.

ISBN 978 1 4202 9393 7

BOXED UP

Fill in the boxes by using the numbers 1, 10, 6 and 3 to make the number sentence true.

$\square - \square + \square = 8 - \square$

Find out if there is more than one answer to the problem.

Extension

Fill in the boxes by using the numbers 7, 3, 8 and 2 to make the number sentence true.

$\square - \square - \square = 10 - \square$

Find out if there is more than one answer to the problem.

Strategy hints!

1 Look for the important words in the question.

9 Think logically.

ISBN 978 1 4202 9393 7

LIGHT BAR LOGIC

Type 4 into your calculator.
You will see that it takes 4 light bars to show this number.

Find the other numbers that have the same number of light bars as the number itself.

Extension

Find a number that is shown on a calculator by 1 less light bar than the number itself.

Strategy hints!

1 Look for the important words in the question.

9 Think logically.

ISBN 978 1 4202 9393 7

LIGHT IT UP

Type 4 into your calculator.
You will see that it takes 4 light bars to show this number.

What is the biggest number that uses 4 light bars when typed into a calculator?

Extension

Find all of the numbers that use 5 light bars when typed into a calculator.

Strategy hints!

1 Look for the important words in the question.

9 Think logically.

ISBN 978 1 4202 9393 7

LIGHT BAR LOOK

Type 17 into your calculator.
You will see that it takes 6 light bars to show this number.

There are 3 other 2-digit numbers that are shown on a calculator by 6 light bars. Find these numbers.

Extension

There is a 3-digit number that uses 6 light bars when shown on a calculator. What is it?

Strategy hints!

1 Look for the important words in the question.

9 Think logically.

ISBN 978 1 4202 9393 7

BEARS AND RABBITS

1 bear and 1 rabbit cost $12.
2 bears and 1 rabbit cost $15.

How much does 1 rabbit cost?

Extension

a) How much do 2 bears and 2 rabbits cost?
b) How much do 3 bears and 5 rabbits cost?

Strategy hints!

1. Look for the important words in the question.
3. Have a go.
9. Think logically.

ISBN 978 1 4202 9393 7

SHIRTS AND SHORTS

1 shirt and 1 pair of shorts cost $20.
1 shirt and 2 pairs of shorts cost $32.

How much does 1 pair of shorts cost?

Extension

a) How much do 2 shirts cost?
b) How much do 2 shirts and 3 pairs of shorts cost?

Strategy hints!

1 Look for the important words in the question.
3 Have a go.
9 Think logically.

ISBN 978 1 4202 9393 7

CARS AND DOLLS

2 toy cars and 1 doll cost \$20.
1 doll costs \$8.

How much does 1 car cost?

Extension

a) How much do 2 cars and 2 dolls cost?
b) How much do 3 cars and 3 dolls cost?

Strategy hints!

1 Look for the important words in the question.
3 Have a go.
9 Think logically.

ISBN 978 1 4202 9393 7

BOOKS AND BOOKMARKS

Grace buys 1 book and 1 bookmark.
Together, they cost $12.
The book costs $6 more than the bookmark.

How much does 1 book cost?

Extension

Make up a problem like this one.

See if a classmate can work it out.

Strategy hints!

1 Look for the important words in the question.

3 Have a go.

9 Think logically.

ISBN 978 1 4202 9393 7

20 CENTS

Sasha has 20 cents in her purse.
There are 4 ways she could make 20 cents.

Find all 4 ways.

Extension

a) Find all the ways Sasha can make 25 cents.
b) Find all the ways Sasha can make 50 cents.

Strategy hints!

1 Look for the important words in the question.
4 Use a table or a chart.
9 Think logically.

ISBN 978 1 4202 9393 7

WHAT NUMBER AM I?

I am in the 10s counting pattern.
I am a 2-digit number.
My digits add up to an odd number.

What is the biggest number I can be?

Extension

Make up a problem like this one.
See if a classmate can work it out.

Strategy hints!

1 Look for the important words in the question.
3 Have a go.
9 Think logically.

ISBN 978 1 4202 9393 7

FIND MY NUMBER

I am a 2-digit number.
My digits add up to 5.

Which 5 numbers can I be?

Extension

Make up a problem like this one.
See if a classmate can work it out.

Strategy hints!

1 Look for the important words in the question.

3 Have a go.

9 Think logically.

ISBN 978 1 4202 9393 7

WHO AM I?

I am a 1-digit number.
On a calculator I have 4, 5 or 6 light bars.
I am an odd number.
I am not 5.

Which 3 numbers can I be?

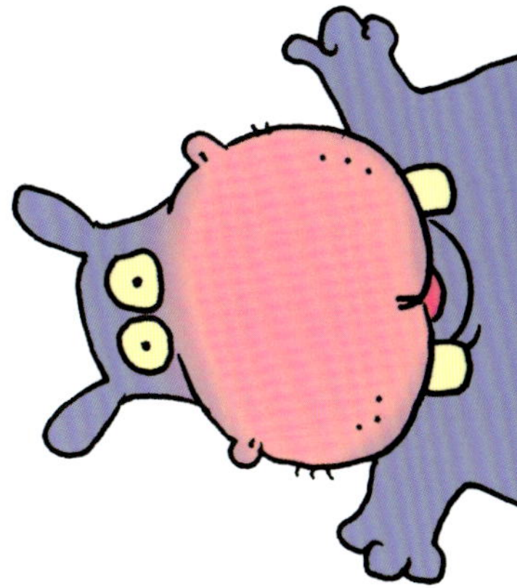

Extension

Make up a problem like this one.
See if a classmate can work it out.

Strategy hints!

1 Look for the important words in the question.

3 Have a go.

9 Think logically.

ISBN 978 1 4202 9393 7

NAME MY NUMBER

I am more than 30 but less than 50.
I am an odd number.
There is a 4 in my number.

List all of the numbers that I can be.

Extension

If I am an even number, which numbers can I be?

Strategy hints!

1 Look for the important words in the question.

3 Have a go.

9 Think logically.

ISBN 978 1 4202 9393 7

GUESS THE DIGITS

I am in the 2s counting pattern.
I am also in the 5s counting pattern.
I am less than 100.
My 2 digits are different by 5.

What number am I?

Extension

If my 2 digits are different by 7, what number am I?

Strategy hints!

1 Look for the important words in the question.
3 Have a go.
9 Think logically.

ISBN 978 1 4202 9393 7

EQUAL ANIMALS

How many echidnas equal a platypus?

Extension

a) How many lyrebirds equal an emu and kangaroo?

b) How many platypuses equal a mob of kangaroos?

Strategy hints!

1 Look for the important words in the question.

9 Think logically.

ISBN 978 1 4202 9393 7

LINE UP PLEASE

Sara is in line outside the classroom.
There are 6 students in front of her.
There are 7 students behind her.

How many students are in the line?

Extension

Line up some coloured counters on the table. Make up a problem like this one.

See if a classmate can work it out.

Strategy hints!

1. Look for the important words in the question.
5. Use a drawing.
8. Make a model.

ISBN 978 1 4202 9393 7

LINE LOGIC

Zac is in line at the canteen.
There are 21 students in the line.
Zac is halfway along the line.

How many students are in front of Zac?

Extension

Line up some coloured counters on the table. Make up a problem like this one.
See if a classmate can work it out.

Strategy hints!

1. Look for the important words in the question.
5. Use a drawing.
8. Make a model.

ISBN 978 1 4202 9393 7

FAIR SHARE

Andrew has 10 stickers.
Tiana has 4 stickers.

How many stickers must Andrew give to Tiana so that they have the same number of stickers each?

Extension

Andrew has 12 stickers and Tiana has 7 stickers.
Can they share them equally?

Strategy hints!

1 Look for the important words in the question.

5 Use a drawing.

8 Make a model.

ISBN 978 1 4202 9393 7

STICKER SHARE

Jess has 8 stickers.
Madison has 1 sticker.
Max has 3 stickers.
They trade stickers. After trading, all 3 children have the same number of stickers.

How many stickers does each child have?

Extension

There are 16 stickers altogether. Can the children share these equally?

Strategy hints!

1. Look for the important words in the question.
5. Use a drawing.
8. Make a model.

ISBN 978 1 4202 9393 7

HOW OLD?

Tom is 7 years old.
Lucy is younger than Jack.
Jack is 2 years younger than Tom.

What is the oldest that Lucy can be?

Extension

Make up a problem like this one.
See if a classmate can work it out.

Strategy hints!

1. Look for the important words in the question.
3. Have a go.
9. Think logically.

ISBN 978 1 4202 9393 7

AGE TO AGE

Ramesh is not as old as Claire.
On his next birthday, Owen will be as old as Ramesh.

List the children from youngest to oldest.

Extension

Claire has an older sister called Kaitlin.
Kaitlin is younger than Owen's big brother Joey.
List the 5 children in order from youngest to oldest.

Strategy hints!

1 Look for the important words in the question.

3 Have a go.

9 Think logically.

ISBN 978 1 4202 9393 7

Focus Number and place value
- Numeration

HOW MANY NUMBERS?

You have the numbers 3, 5 and 8.

Use these numbers to make as many 2-digit numbers as you can.

Extension

Try using 7, 8 and 1. Will the number of answers be the same?

Strategy hints!

1. Look for the important words in the question.
9. Think logically.

ISBN 978 1 4202 9393 7

NUMBERS UP

You have the numbers 2, 7 and 2.

Use these numbers to make as many possible 2-digit numbers as you can.

Extension

Try using 4, 8 and 8. Will the number of answers be the same?

Strategy hints!

1 Look for the important words in the question.

9 Think logically.

ISBN 978 1 4202 9393 7

TARGET TIME

Rohan fires 3 arrows at this target.

Rohan's score is 15.

How might Rohan's arrows have landed on the target?

Extension

Next time, Rohan misses with 1 of his arrows. What is the biggest score Rohan can make with the 2 arrows that are left?

Strategy hints!

1 Look for the important words in the question.

5 Use a drawing.

9 Think logically.

ISBN 978 1 4202 9393 7

AIM THE ARROW

Samira fires 3 arrows at this target.

Samira's score is the 2nd highest possible score.

How have Samira's arrows landed?

Extension

Next time Samira fires 3 arrows at the target, her arrows all score points. She scores the 2nd lowest possible score with her 3 arrows. How have Samira's arrows landed?

Strategy hints!

1 Look for the important words in the question.

5 Use a drawing.

9 Think logically.

ISBN 978 1 4202 9393 7

FUNNY NUMBERS

Between 1 and 100, there are 4 numbers where the 10s digit is half the 1s digit.

Find these 4 numbers.

Extension

Between 1 and 100, there are 4 numbers where the 1s digit is half the 10s digit. Find these 4 numbers.

Strategy hints!

1 Look for the important words in the question.

2 Look for a pattern.

9 Think logically.

ISBN 978 1 4202 9393 7

UNIQUE NUMBERS

Between 1 and 100, there are 9 numbers where the 10s digit added to the 1s digit equals 9.

Find these 9 numbers.

Extension

Between 1 and 100, there are 8 numbers where the 10s digit added to the 1s digit equals 8. Find these 8 numbers.

Strategy hints!

1. Look for the important words in the question.
2. Look for a pattern.
9. Think logically.

ISBN 978 1 4202 9393 7

ALL THE TWOS

Emma writes down all of the numbers from 1 to 30.

How many times does she write '2'?

This table will help.

	1 to 10	11 to 20	21 to 30
Number of 2s			

Extension

Emma then writes down all of the numbers from 31 to 60.
How many times does she write '5'?

Strategy hints!

1 Look for the important words in the question.

2 Look for a pattern.

4 Use a table or a chart.

ISBN 978 1 4202 9393 7

ALL THE NUMBERS

Anastasia writes down all of the numbers from 1 to 20.
How many digits does she use? (Remember that 5 is a 1-digit number and that 15 is a 2-digit number.)

This table will help.

	1 to 9	10 to 20
Number of digits		

Extension

Anastasia then writes down all of the numbers from 21 to 30. How many digits does she write?

Strategy hints!

1 Look for the important words in the question.
2 Look for a pattern.
4 Use a table or a chart.

ISBN 978 1 4202 9393 7

WHERE DID HE START?

Lucas spends \$5, then spends \$3, then spends \$4. He has \$10 left over.

How much money did Lucas have to begin with?

Extension

Make up a problem like this one.

See if a classmate can work it out.

Strategy hints!

1 Look for the important words in the question.

6 Work backwards.

ISBN 978 1 4202 9393 7

MONEY SHARE

Sanjay gives half of his money to Georgia. He has $3 left over.

How much money did Sanjay have to begin with?

Extension

Sanjay gives half of his money to Georgia. He then spends $1. He has $3 left over. How much money did Sanjay have to begin with?

Strategy hints!

1 Look for the important words in the question.

6 Work backwards.

ISBN 978 1 4202 9393 7

HOW MUCH MONEY?

Deniz spends $10. Then he gives half of his money to Milly. He has $3 left over.

How much money did Deniz have to begin with?

Extension

Make up a problem like this one.
See if a classmate can work it out.

Strategy hints!

1. Look for the important words in the question.
6. Work backwards.

ISBN 978 1 4202 9393 7

COLUMN CRAFT

Numbers have been put into certain columns in a chart.

What type of numbers are in column A?
What type of numbers are in column B?
What type of numbers are in column C?

A	B	C
35	14	20
75	90	50
90	78	80
25	30	60
40	98	90

Extension

a) Why is 90 in all 3 columns?

b) How many numbers, less than 100, could be in all 3 columns?

Strategy hints!

1. Look for the important words in the question.
2. Look for a pattern.
4. Use a table or a chart.

ISBN 978 1 4202 9393 7

CRAZY COLUMNS

Numbers have been put into certain columns in a chart.

Eric has put a number in column A that should be in column B, and a number in column B that should be in column A.

Which numbers should Eric switch?

A	B
71	14
45	90
92	78
25	30
41	93

Extension

If you could put 3-digit numbers in the columns, what are the 2 biggest possible numbers in each column?

Strategy hints!

1 Look for the important words in the question.
2 Look for a pattern.
4 Use a table or a chart.

ISBN 978 1 4202 9393 7

ODD ONE OUT

Which of these numbers is the ‘odd one out’?

26, 7, 54, 18, 64

Extension

Find a reason why each of these numbers could be the ‘odd one out’.

22, 107, 40, 56

Strategy hints!

1. Look for the important words in the question.
2. Look for a pattern.

ISBN 978 1 4202 9393 7

40 CENTS

Isla has 40 cents in her purse.
Isla has only 7 coins.

Which coins are in Isla's purse?

Extension

Using only 10 cent and 20 cent coins, find all the ways you can make 40 cents.

Strategy hints!

1 Look for the important words in the question.

9 Think logically.

ISBN 978 1 4202 9393 7

MAGIC SQUARE

Finish this magic square.
You will need to use all of the numbers from 1 to 9.
Each line must add up to 15.

8		6
3	5	
	9	

Extension

Find another way to arrange the numbers in the magic square. Use the numbers 1 to 9. Each line must add up to 15.

Strategy hints!

1. Look for the important words in the question.
2. Look for a pattern.
3. Have a go.

ISBN 978 1 4202 9393 7

BACKWARDS AND FORWARDS

Look for a quick way to find the answer to this question.

6 + 5 – 6 + 4 – 5 – 4

Extension

Look for a quick way to find the answer to this question.

25 + 13 + 30 – 25 – 30 – 13

Strategy hints!

1 Look for the important words in the question.

7 Try an easier problem.

9 Think logically.

ISBN 978 1 4202 9393 7

LETTERBOXES

The houses on my side of the street are all odd numbers. The houses on the other side of the street are all even numbers.
My letterbox is number 17.
My neighbour on one side has letterbox number 19.
There are 2 more houses in my street after my next door neighbour.

How many houses are on my side of the street?

Extension

How many houses in the street have even, 2-digit numbers on their letterboxes?
List these house numbers in order.

Strategy hints!

1. Look for the important words in the question.
2. Look for a pattern.

ISBN 978 1 4202 9393 7

STREET NUMBERS

My grandma lives on a short street. Houses on my grandma's side of the street are all odd numbers. The houses on the other side of the street are all even numbers.

Grandma's house is number 7.

Her house is exactly halfway along the street.

How many houses are on Grandma's side of the street?

Extension

The numbers on one side of a street go up to 21.
Which house number is exactly halfway along that side of the street?

Strategy hints!

1. Look for the important words in the question.
2. Look for a pattern.

ISBN 978 1 4202 9393 7

NEED A LIFT?

I enter a lift at level 3.

I go up 4 levels.

I then go down 5 levels.

Then the lift breaks down and I have to walk down to the ground floor.

How many levels do I have to walk down?

Extension

Make up a problem like this one.

See if a classmate can work it out.

Strategy hints!

1 Look for the important words in the question.

3 Have a go.

9 Think logically.

ISBN 978 1 4202 9393 7

LIFT ME HIGHER

I enter a lift at level 5.
The lift goes up 1 level and then down 2 levels over and over again.

How many times will this happen before I am at the ground floor?

Extension

I enter a lift at level 25.
The lift goes up 1 level and then down 2 levels over and over again.
How many times will this happen before I am at the ground floor?

Strategy hints!

1. Look for the important words in the question.
3. Have a go.
9. Think logically.

ISBN 978 1 4202 9393 7

CONSECUTIVE CHALLENGE

Numbers that are next to each other, like 2 and 3, are called consecutive numbers.

Which 2 consecutive numbers add up to 17?

Extension

a) Which 2 consecutive numbers add up to 31?

b) Which 2 consecutive numbers add up to 53?

Strategy hints!

1 Look for the important words in the question.

3 Have a go.

9 Think logically.

ISBN 978 1 4202 9393 7

NUMBER NEIGHBOURS

Numbers that are next to each other, like 2 and 3, are called consecutive numbers.

Which 3 consecutive numbers add up to 18?

Extension

a) Which 3 consecutive numbers add up to 30?

b) Which 3 consecutive numbers add up to 45?

Strategy hints!

1 Look for the important words in the question.

3 Have a go.

9 Think logically.

ISBN 978 1 4202 9393 7

LEG WORK

I have 3 pets. Altogether, they have 10 legs.
My pets could be dogs or birds.

a) How many pet dogs do I have?

b) How many pet birds do I have?

Extension

I have 3 pets. Altogether, they have 20 legs.
My pets could be ladybirds or spiders.

a) How many pet ladybirds do I have?

b) How many pet spiders do I have?

Strategy hints!

1 Look for the important words in the question.

3 Have a go.

9 Think logically.

ISBN 978 1 4202 9393 7

PAWS AND CLAWS

I have 5 pets. Altogether, they have 14 legs.
My pets could be cats or chickens.

a) How many pet cats do I have?

b) How many pet chickens do I have?

Extension

Make up a problem like this one.
See if a classmate can work it out.

Strategy hints!

1 Look for the important words in the question.

3 Have a go.

9 Think logically.

ISBN 978 1 4202 9393 7

BIRTHDAY BONANZA

Abbey is given $1 on her 1st birthday, $2 on her 2nd birthday, $4 on her 3rd birthday and $8 on her 4th birthday.

a) What is happening to her presents?

b) How much does Abbey get on her 5th birthday?

Extension

a) How old is Abbey when she is given $32?

b) How old is Abbey when she is given $128?

Strategy hints!

1 Look for the important words in the question.

2 Look for a pattern.

9 Think logically.

ISBN 978 1 4202 9393 7

NUMBER CRUNCHER

'Ten' uses 3 letters, not 10 letters.
'Seven' uses 5 letters, not 7 letters.

What is the only number that uses the same number of letters as the number itself?

Extension

What numbers and their letters are only 1 apart?

Strategy hints!

1. Look for the important words in the question.
9. Think logically.

ISBN 978 1 4202 9393 7

WHICH COLUMN?

In which columns will these numbers be found?

a) 10
b) 20
c) 30
d) 40

A	B	C	D
1	2	3	4
8	7	6	5

Extension

In which columns will 50 and 60 be found?

Strategy hints!

1 Look for the important words in the question.
2 Look for a pattern.
4 Use a table or a chart.

ISBN 978 1 4202 9393 7

NUMBER COLUMNS

In which columns will these numbers be found?

a) 9
b) 10
c) 11
d) 12
e) 13

A	B	C	D
1	3	2	4
5	7	6	8

Extension

In which column will 20 be found?

Strategy hints!

1 Look for the important words in the question.
2 Look for a pattern.
4 Use a table or a chart.

ISBN 978 1 4202 9393 7

FOLLOW THE SYMBOLS

The symbol @ means add on 2.
The symbol ^ means add on 3.
The symbol * means take away 1.

Start at 10. Then, * ^ ^ @ *
What is the answer?

Extension

After you ^ * * @ @ you are at the number 20.
Where did you start?

Strategy hints!

1 Look for the important words in the question.
2 Look for a pattern.
6 Work backwards.

ISBN 978 1 4202 9393 7

MISSING NUMBER

3 numbers add up to 20.
1 of the numbers is 6.
1 of the numbers is 5.

What is the other number?

Extension

4 numbers add up to 20.
1 of the numbers is 3.
1 of the numbers is 8.
What do the other 2 numbers add up to?

Strategy hints!

1 Look for the important words in the question.
6 Work backwards.
9 Think logically.

ISBN 978 1 4202 9393 7

TWO BOXES THE SAME

a) 12 = ☐ + ☐

The numbers in the boxes are the same. What number is in the boxes?

b) 12 = ☐ + ☐ + ☐

The numbers in the boxes are the same. What number is in the boxes?

c) 12 = ☐ + ☐ + ☐ + ☐

The numbers in the boxes are the same. What number is in the boxes?

Extension

What can the answers to question **a)** be if the boxes contain 2 different numbers?

See how many answers you can find.

Strategy hints!

1 Look for the important words in the question.

9 Think logically.

ISBN 978 1 4202 9393 7

DIFFERENT AGES

The ages of Otto and Laura add up to 20.
Otto is older than Laura.

What is the oldest that Laura can be?

Extension

If both children are an even number of years old, what is the oldest that Otto can be?

Strategy hints!

1 Look for the important words in the question.

9 Think logically.

ISBN 978 1 4202 9393 7

FIND THE AGES

Raheel's age minus Kim's age equals 5 years.
Raheel is younger than 12.
Raheel's age is an even number.

How old can Raheel be?
There are 3 possible answers.

Extension

Is Kim's age an even or an odd number?

Strategy hints!

1 Look for the important words in the question.

9 Think logically.

ISBN 978 1 4202 9393 7

WHAT IF?

If 1 were 3.
If 2 were 4.
If 3 were 5.

What would 2 + 3 − 1 equal?

Extension

Make up a problem like this one.
See if a classmate can work it out.

Strategy hints!

1 Look for the important words in the question.
9 Think logically.

ISBN 978 1 4202 9393 7

ALL ABOUT BETH

Beth never tells the truth.

Beth says she is 7.

Beth says she is older than 10.

Beth says her age is an even number.

What is the oldest that Beth can be?

Extension

Make up a problem like this one.

See if a classmate can work it out.

Strategy hints!

1 Look for the important words in the question.

9 Think logically.

ISBN 978 1 4202 9393 7

50 CENTS

Keira has 4 coins. She only has 2 different types of coins.
She has 50 cents altogether.

What 4 coins does Keira have?

Extension

What is the biggest amount of money Keira can have with 4 coins?

Strategy hints!

1. Look for the important words in the question.
9. Think logically.

ISBN 978 1 4202 9393 7

DIFFERENT NUMBERS

2 numbers add up to 100.
They are different numbers.
They are 4 apart.

What numbers are they?

Extension

2 numbers add up to 100.
They are different numbers.
They are as far apart as possible.
What numbers are they?

Strategy hints!

1 Look for the important words in the question.

9 Think logically.

ISBN 978 1 4202 9393 7

GRANDMA AND GRANDAD

My grandma is 85.
My grandad is older than my grandma.
He will be 100 in less than 10 years.

What is the youngest that Grandad could be?

Extension

When Grandad is 94, Grandma will be 88. How old was Grandad when Grandma was born?

Strategy hints!

1 Look for the important words in the question.
9 Think logically.

ISBN 978 1 4202 9393 7

SHOPPING

I bought a book for $10 and a soft toy for $9. I got $11 in change.

a) How much money did I take shopping?

b) My change came in 6 coins.
What coins were in my change?

Extension

Make up a problem like this one.
See if a classmate can work it out.

Strategy hints!

1. Look for the important words in the question.
6. Work backwards.
9. Think logically.

ISBN 978 1 4202 9393 7

SHOE SIZE

My shoe size is a number name that has 4 letters in it.
It is in the 3s counting pattern.

What size is my shoe?

Extension

Find your shoe size. Make up a problem like this one about it.

See if a classmate can work it out.

Strategy hints!

1. Look for the important words in the question.
9. Think logically.

ISBN 978 1 4202 9393 7

NUMBERS LINE UP

3 numbers on a number line are added up.
These numbers are next to each other.
The middle number is 5.

What do the 3 numbers add up to?

Extension

3 numbers on a number line are added up. These numbers are next to each other. They add up to 21. What are the 3 numbers?

Strategy hints!

1 Look for the important words in the question.

9 Think logically.

ISBN 978 1 4202 9393 7

BON AND BEN

Bon and Ben's ages, when added up, equal 12 years.
Bon is Ben's older sister.

How old can Ben be?

Extension

In 5 years, what will Bon and Ben's ages add up to?

Strategy hints!

1 Look for the important words in the question.

9 Think logically.

ISBN 978 1 4202 9393 7

EGYPTIAN NUMERALS

In Ancient Egypt people counted like this:

I = 1   I I = 2   I I I = 3   I I I I = 4

∩ = 10   ∩∩ = 20   ∩∩∩ = 30   ∩∩∩∩ = 40

For example, I I I∩ = 13.

What did ∩I I∩ I stand for?

Extension

Make up new symbols for numbers from 1 to 10 and from 10 to 100. Then, write some problems using the symbols. See if a classmate can work them out.

Strategy hints!

1. Look for the important words in the question.
2. Look for a pattern.
9. Think logically.

ISBN 978 1 4202 9393 7

ALIEN NUMERALS

On the planet Bognat the aliens count like this:

[*] = 1, [* *] = 2, [* * *] = 3, [^] = 4, [^^] = 5, [^^^] = 6,
[#] = 7, [##] = 8 and [###] = 9

Find the answer to [* *] + [^^] + [#]

Extension

Make up symbols that could be used on Bognat for 10, 11 and 12. Then, write some problems using all the symbols. See if a classmate can work them out.

Strategy hints!

1 Look for the important words in the question.
2 Look for a pattern.
9 Think logically.

ISBN 978 1 4202 9393 7

2-DIGIT NUMBERS

Find the 3rd biggest 2-digit number.
Now find the smallest 2-digit number.

Take the smaller number away from the bigger number. What is left over?

Extension

Take away the 2nd smallest 2-digit number from the 2nd biggest 2-digit number. What do you notice?

Strategy hints!

1 Look for the important words in the question.

9 Think logically.

ISBN 978 1 4202 9393 7

DIFFERENT DIGITS

2 different 2-digit numbers are placed side by side.
They both use the same 2 numbers, like 17 and 71.
The difference between the 2 different 2-digit numbers is as small as it can be.

What could the 2 numbers be?
There is more than one possible answer.

Extension

2 different 2-digit numbers are placed side by side.
They both use the same 2 numbers, like 17 and 71.
They are as far apart in size as they can be.
What are the numbers?

Strategy hints!

1 Look for the important words in the question.

9 Think logically.

ISBN 978 1 4202 9393 7

TOY SALE

Sami bought some toys at a sale.
These toys were for sale.

Sami spent 55 cents and bought 4 toys.

What did Sami buy?

Extension

See if you can find more than one answer that works.

Strategy hints!

1 Look for the important words in the question.

5 Use a drawing.

9 Think logically.

ISBN 978 1 4202 9393 7

MAIN TOWN

Main Town is halfway between Ambley and Gotley.
Ambley and Gotley are 24 kilometres apart.

How far apart are Ambley and Main Town?

Extension

The town of Clarke is halfway between Main Town and Gotley. Draw a map showing these 4 towns and how far apart they are.

Strategy hints!

1 Look for the important words in the question.

5 Use a drawing.

9 Think logically.

ISBN 978 1 4202 9393 7

Focus Number and place value
- Addition
- Subtraction

COLOURED PENCILS

My pencil case has 10 red, 5 blue and 16 green pencils.
It has 40 pencils altogether.

How many of my coloured pencils are not red, blue or green?

Extension

The other pencils are yellow and orange.
I have more yellow than orange pencils.
How many yellow pencils could I have in the pencil case?

Strategy hints!

1. Look for the important words in the question.
9. Think logically.

ISBN 978 1 4202 9393 7

COUNTING IN THREES

Zafar started at 2 and skip counted in 3s like this:

2, 5, 8, 11 . . .

Will 30 be in this pattern?

Extension

What will be the closest number to 60 in this pattern?

Strategy hints!

1 Look for the important words in the question.

2 Look for a pattern.

9 Think logically.

ISBN 978 1 4202 9393 7

BIG TOWN

In Big Town, every number is doubled.
For example, 1 = 2, 2 = 4 and 3 = 6

In Big Town what does 5 + 4 – 1 equal?

Extension

Make up a Big Town number sentence.
See if a classmate can work it out.

Strategy hints!

1. Look for the important words in the question.
2. Look for a pattern.
9. Think logically.

ISBN 978 1 4202 9393 7

RACE PLACE

In a running race, Alana came 1st, Freya came 2nd and Chloe came 3rd. Chloe beat 18 other runners.

How many people were in the race?

Extension

Emma finished 5th.

a) How many runners beat Emma?

b) How many runners did Emma beat?

Strategy hints!

1 Look for the important words in the question.

5 Use a drawing.

9 Think logically.

ISBN 978 1 4202 9393 7

UP TO 20

Think of the numbers 1, 2, 3, 4, 5, 6, 7, 8, 9 and 10.

Starting at 1, how many of these do you need to add to each other to reach 20?

Extension

a) Starting at 1, how many numbers do you need to add to each other to reach 36?

b) What is the total of the last 4 numbers?

Strategy hints!

1 Look for the important words in the question.

9 Think logically.

ISBN 978 1 4202 9393 7

20 PLUS

4 numbers add up to 20.
2 of the numbers are 5 and 6.

What is the biggest number that 1 of the other 2 numbers can be?

Extension

4 numbers add up to 20.
What is the biggest that 1 of the numbers can be?

Strategy hints!

1 Look for the important words in the question.

9 Think logically.

ISBN 978 1 4202 9393 7

EVEN STEVEN

Steven skip counts in 2s up to 40.

How many numbers does he count?

Extension

Steven starts at 1 and skip counts in 2s up to 39.
How many numbers does he count?

Strategy hints!

1. Look for the important words in the question.
2. Look for a pattern.
9. Think logically.

ISBN 978 1 4202 9393 7

BOX PUZZLE

Use the numbers 1, 3, 4 and 6 to make this true:

$$
\begin{array}{rcc}
 & \square & \square \\
+ & & \square \\
+ & & \square \\
\hline
 & 4 & 1 \\
\hline
\end{array}
$$

Extension

Make up a problem like this one.

See if a classmate can work it out.

Strategy hints!

1 Look for the important words in the question.

2 Look for a pattern.

9 Think logically.

ISBN 978 1 4202 9393 7

MANY WAYS

One way of making 20 is:

10 + 9 + 1

Find all the other ways you can make 20 by adding 2 numbers to 10.

Extension

Make 2 sums. Each sum must equal 20. Each sum must contain 3 numbers that are the same and 1 number that is different.

Strategy hints!

1. Look for the important words in the question.
2. Look for a pattern.
9. Think logically.

ISBN 978 1 4202 9393 7

NUMBER THINKING

I am a 2-digit number.
I am less than 60.
I am in the 2s counting pattern.
I am also in the 5s counting pattern.

What is the biggest number I can be?

Extension

I am a 2-digit number.
I am between 50 and 80.
I am not in the 2s counting pattern.
I am not in the 5s counting pattern.
My 2 digits are different.
What are the biggest 3 numbers I can be?

Strategy hints!

1 Look for the important words in the question.
2 Look for a pattern.
9 Think logically.

ISBN 978 1 4202 9393 7

ADDING UP

a) 2 numbers add up to 13.
The numbers are 3 apart.
What are the 2 numbers?

b) 2 numbers add up to 19.
The numbers are 9 apart.
What are the 2 numbers?

Extension

Make up a problem like this that uses the number 11.
See if a classmate can work it out.

Strategy hints!

1. Look for the important words in the question.
2. Look for a pattern.
3. Have a go.

ISBN 978 1 4202 9393 7

20 PUZZLE

2 numbers add up to 20.
Both numbers are bigger than 3.
Both numbers are even numbers.

What can the numbers be?

Extension

2 numbers add up to 30.
Both numbers are smaller than 16.
Both numbers are odd numbers.
What are the numbers?

Strategy hints!

1 Look for the important words in the question.
3 Have a go.
9 Think logically.

ISBN 978 1 4202 9393 7

CALCULATOR MIX-UP

Gemma wants to type 6 + 4 into her calculator.
Gemma makes a mistake and types – instead of +.

How far from the correct answer is the number on Gemma's screen?

Extension

Gemma wants to type 6 + 4 + 5 into her calculator.
Gemma makes a mistake and types 6 + 4 – 5.
How far from the correct answer is the number on Gemma's screen?

Strategy hints!

1 Look for the important words in the question.

9 Think logically.

ISBN 978 1 4202 9393 7

Focus Number and place value
- Addition
- Subtraction

STAMP SALE

Asta buys a stamp for $10.
She then sells it for $13.
Later, Asta buys a drink for $2.

How much money does Asta have left?

Extension

Stamps cost $2 each.
It costs $11 to post a parcel. How many stamps do you need to buy to post a parcel?

Strategy hints!

1 Look for the important words in the question.

9 Think logically.

ISBN 978 1 4202 9393 7

MISSING NUMBER

Find the missing number in this sum.

5 + 5 + 8 + ? + 6 + 4 = 30

Extension

Use the same pattern to find the missing numbers in this sum.

9 + ? + 2 + ? = 20

Strategy hints!

1. Look for the important words in the question.
2. Look for a pattern.

ISBN 978 1 4202 9393 7

CLOSE TO 35

Start at 3 and skip count in 5s like this:
3, 8, 13 . . .

What is the closest number to 35 that you will count?

Extension

a) Will 58 be in this pattern?
b) Will 112 be in this pattern?

Strategy hints!

1. Look for the important words in the question.
2. Look for a pattern.

ISBN 978 1 4202 9393 7

ADD TO ITSELF

a) What number, when added to itself, equals 8 + 2?

☐ + ☐ = 8 + 2

b) What number, when added to itself, equals 20 + 6?

☐ + ☐ = 20 + 6

Extension

a) What number, when added to itself, equals 10 – 2?

☐ + ☐ = 10 – 2

b) What number, when added to itself, equals 20 – 4?

☐ + ☐ = 20 – 4

Strategy hints!

1. Look for the important words in the question.
2. Have a go.

ISBN 978 1 4202 9393 7

DOUBLE UP

a) What number, when added to itself, is close to 15?

☐ + ☐ = about 15

b) What number, when added to itself, is close to 25?

☐ + ☐ = about 25

There can be more than one answer.

Extension

a) What number, when added to itself, equals about 31?

☐ + ☐ = about 31

b) What number, when added to itself, equals about 101?

☐ + ☐ = about 101

There can be more than one answer.

Strategy hints!

1 Look for the important words in the question.

3 Have a go.

ISBN 978 1 4202 9393 7

OPEN BOOK

I open up a book.
The 2 pages that I open add up to 21.

What pages is the book open to?

Extension

Can the 2 pages add up to 20?

Strategy hints!

1 Look for the important words in the question.

3 Have a go.

9 Think logically.

ISBN 978 1 4202 9393 7

HALFWAY THROUGH

a) I open up my book.
I have just read page 30.
I see that I am halfway through the book.
How many pages are in the book?

b) My brother is also halfway through his book. He is on page 52.
How many pages are in his book?

Extension

I open up a different book.
I have just read page 20.
I see that I am 6 pages away from having read half of the book.
How many pages are in the book?

Strategy hints!

1 Look for the important words in the question.
3 Have a go.
9 Think logically.

ISBN 978 1 4202 9393 7

2 BOOKS HIGH

2 books are on a table on top of each other.
1 book is twice as thick as the other book.
Together, the books are 6 centimetres thick.

How thick are the 2 books?

Extension

2 books are on a table on top of each other.
1 book is twice as thick as the other book.
Together, the books are 15 centimetres thick.
How thick are the 2 books?

Strategy hints!

1 Look for the important words in the question.
3 Have a go.
9 Think logically.

ISBN 978 1 4202 9393 7

MEASUREMENT AND GEOMETRY

PENCILS AND RULERS

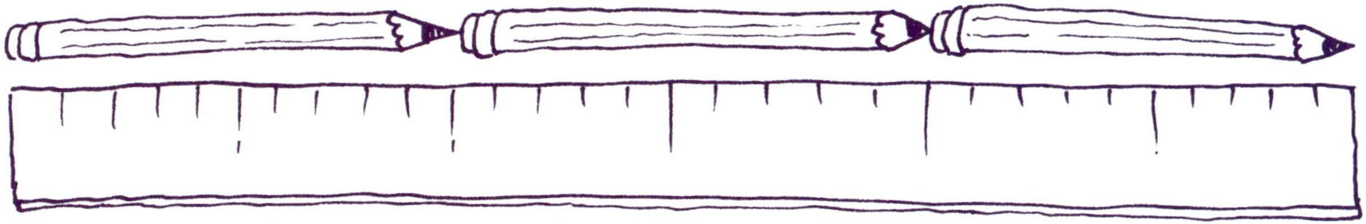

How many rulers will be the same length as 12 pencils?

Extension

Four pencils are the same length as 1 ruler.
How many pencils will be the same length as 9 rulers?

Strategy hints!

1 Look for the important words in the question.

5 Use a drawing.

9 Think logically.

ISBN 978 1 4202 9393 7

PAINTS AND PAINTBRUSHES

How many paintbrushes will it take to go past the length of 7 tubes of paint?

Extension

Three erasers are the same length as 2 tubes of paint. How many erasers are the same length as 3 paintbrushes?

Strategy hints!

1 Look for the important words in the question.

5 Use a drawing.

9 Think logically.

ISBN 978 1 4202 9393 7

BLOCKS FOR SALE

Each block costs $2.

How much does it cost to buy these blocks?

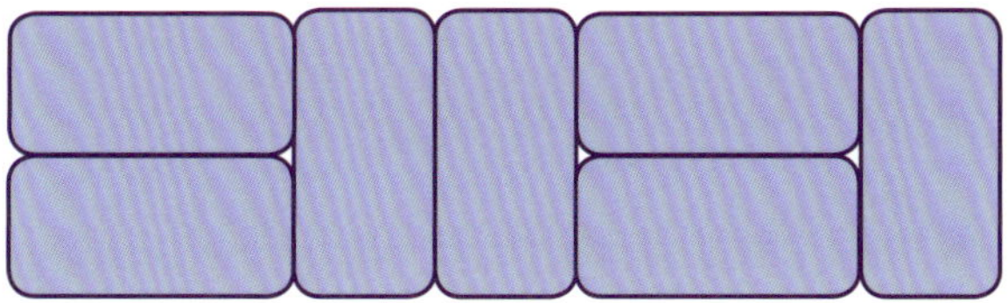

Extension

a) How many blocks can you buy for $26?

b) How many blocks can you buy for $40?

Strategy hints!

1 Look for the important words in the question.

5 Use a drawing.

9 Think logically.

ISBN 978 1 4202 9393 7

INSECT LENGTHS

A bee is longer than an ant.
A wasp is longer than a bee.
A flea is shorter than an ant.

List the 4 insects in order from shortest to longest.

Extension

Make up a problem like this one. List 6 animals in order from shortest to longest.

Strategy hints!

1 Look for the important words in the question.

5 Use a drawing.

9 Think logically.

ISBN 978 1 4202 9393 7

ALL THE TRIANGLES

How many triangles can you see in the picture?

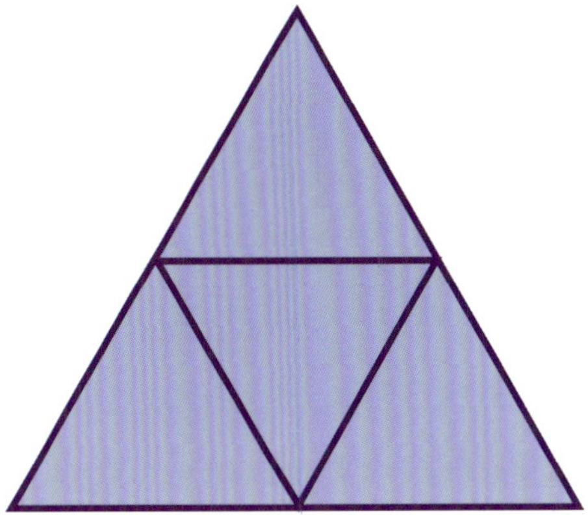

Extension

Imagine the triangle has another layer at the bottom. How many little triangles would be in the bottom layer?

Strategy hints!

1 Look for the important words in the question.

5 Use a drawing.

9 Think logically.

ISBN 978 1 4202 9393 7

ALL THE SQUARES

How many squares can you see?

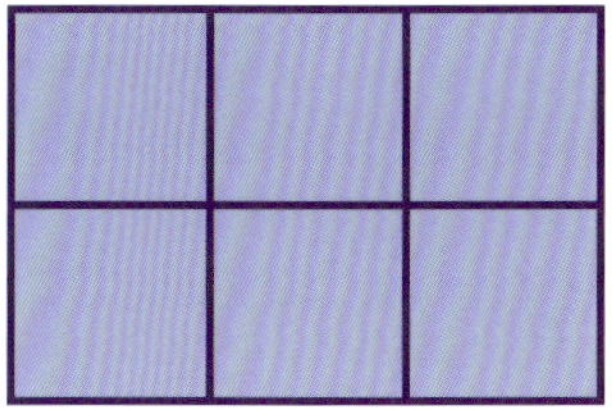

Extension

How many squares can you see?

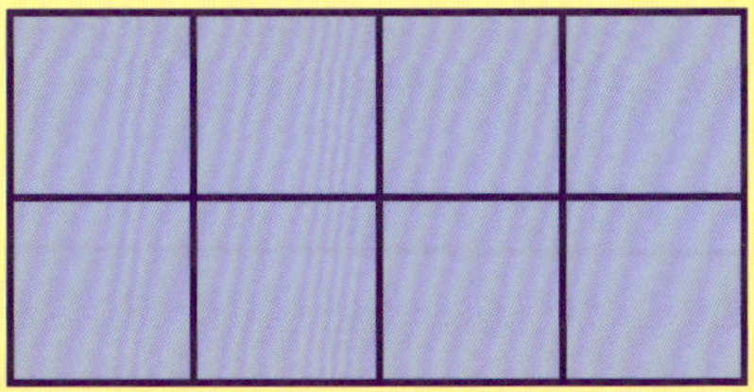

Strategy hints!

1 Look for the important words in the question.

5 Use a drawing.

9 Think logically.

ISBN 978 1 4202 9393 7

TRAINING

Ravi trains with his soccer club on Mondays that are even days of the month and on Thursdays that are odd days of the month.
Ravi has a calendar to work out when he will train.

S	M	T	W	T	F	S
		1	2	3	4	5
6	7	8	9	10	11	12
13	14	15	16	17	18	19
20	21	22	23	24	25	26
27	28	29	30	31		

How many days will Ravi train this month?

Extension

There are 7 months that this calendar could show. The calendar shows the 6th of these months. Which month is shown on the calendar?

Strategy hints!

1 Look for the important words in the question.
4 Use a table or a chart.
9 Think logically.

ISBN 978 1 4202 9393 7

TIME PATTERN

Here is a pattern to do with time.

J, F, M, A, M, J, ☐, ☐, ☐

Fill in the gaps in the pattern.

Extension

F will appear again in this pattern.
In which position will F appear for the 2nd time?

Strategy hints!

1. Look for the important words in the question.
2. Look for a pattern.
9. Think logically.

ISBN 978 1 4202 9393 7

V SHAPE

In which of these pictures can you see the letter V?

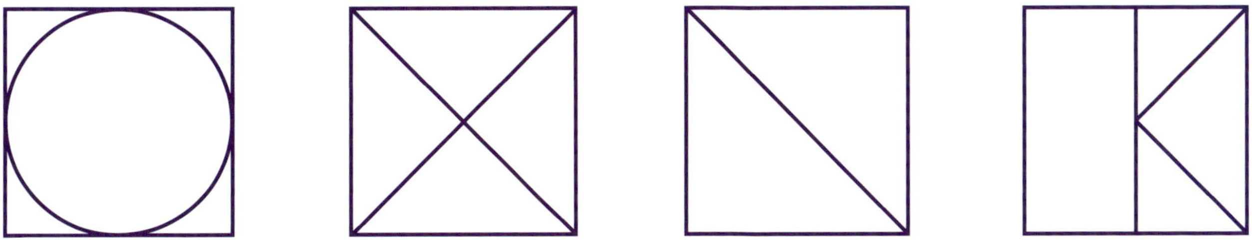

A B C D

Extension

In which of the pictures can you see 3 triangles and 2 rectangles?

Strategy hints!

1 Look for the important words in the question.

5 Use a drawing.

9 Think logically.

ISBN 978 1 4202 9393 7

MISSING PARTS

This shape has some blocks missing.

How many blocks need to be added to finish it off?

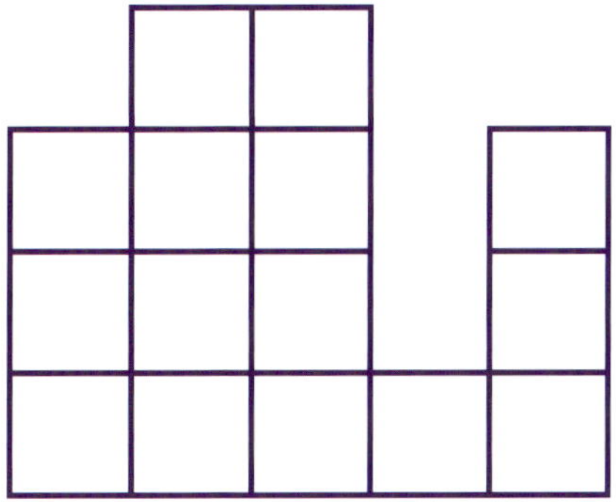

Extension

How many more blocks need to be added to the shape to make it a square?

Strategy hints!

1 Look for the important words in the question.

5 Use a drawing.

9 Think logically.

ISBN 978 1 4202 9393 7

PAPER CUT

Nathan folds a piece of paper in half and then cuts out a piece.

What will the piece of paper look like when he unfolds it?

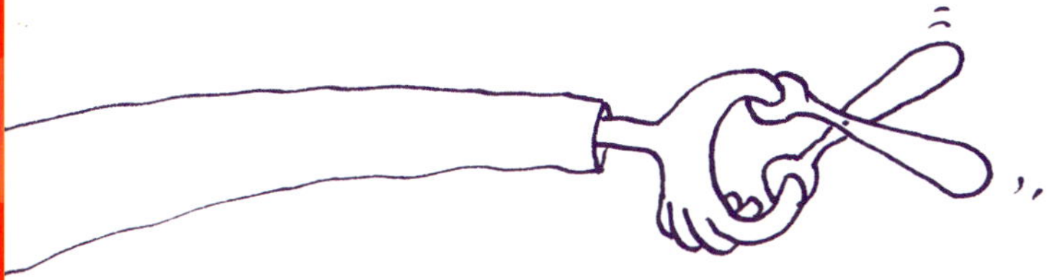

Extension

Fold a piece of paper in half and make a cut in it.
Predict what the paper will look like when it is unfolded.

Strategy hints!

1 Look for the important words in the question.

5 Use a drawing.

8 Make a model.

ISBN 978 1 4202 9393 7

CORNERS, EDGES, FACES

Get 2 connecting blocks and clip them together.

Look at the shape you have made. Does it have more corners, more edges, or more faces?

Remember, count the face with the connector as one face.

Extension

Clip 2 more connecting blocks on top of this shape.

Count the corners, edges and faces.

What do you notice?

Strategy hints!

1 Look for the important words in the question.

8 Make a model.

ISBN 978 1 4202 9393 7

DIGITAL CHALLENGE

How many light bars does a digital clock use to show half past 1?

Extension

How many light bars will the clock use to show the time an hour later?

Strategy hints!

1 Look for the important words in the question.

5 Use a drawing.

ISBN 978 1 4202 9393 7

HANDY HANDS

A clock has the big hand on 6.
The little hand is halfway between 3 and 4.

What is the time?

Extension

What will the time be one and a half hours later?

Strategy hints!

1 Look for the important words in the question.

5 Use a drawing.

8 Make a model.

ISBN 978 1 4202 9393 7

ARROWHEADS

↑	→	↓	←	?
1	2	3	4	5

a) What comes 5th in this pattern?

b) What comes 7th in this pattern?

Extension

a) What comes 13th in this pattern?

b) What comes 20th in this pattern?

Strategy hints!

1. Look for the important words in the question.
2. Look for a pattern.
5. Use a drawing.

ISBN 978 1 4202 9393 7

NETBALL TIMES

This clock shows when Ella's netball game starts.

This shows when Ella's netball game finishes.

How long does her game last?

Extension

When Ella gets home, her digital watch shows 12:00. How long, in minutes, did it take Ella to get home after the game?

Strategy hints!

1 Look for the important words in the question.

5 Use a drawing.

ISBN 978 1 4202 9393 7

KARATE TRAINING

The calendar shows part of a month and the days that Weng trains for Karate.

S	M	T	W	T	F	S
				1	2	3
4	(K)	6	7	8	9	(K)
11	12	13	14	(K)	16	17
18	19	(K)	21	22	23	

What are the next 2 dates in this month that Weng will train?

Extension

How can you tell that this month is not February?

Strategy hints!

1. Look for the important words in the question.
4. Use a table or a chart.

ISBN 978 1 4202 9393 7

NOT LIKE THE OTHERS

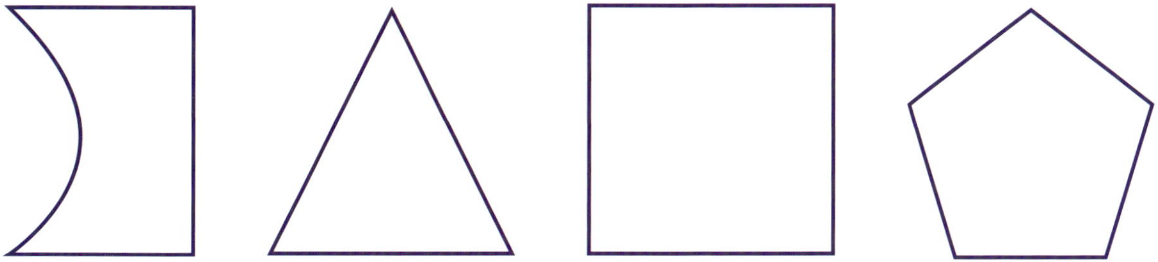

A B C D

Which shape is not like the others?

Extension

Make up a pattern like this one with an odd one out.
See if a classmate can find the odd one out.

Strategy hints!

1 Look for the important words in the question.

5 Use a drawing.

9 Think logically.

ISBN 978 1 4202 9393 7

EQUAL GLASSES

Ruby pours juice into 3 glasses.
She wants to make the glasses all equal.

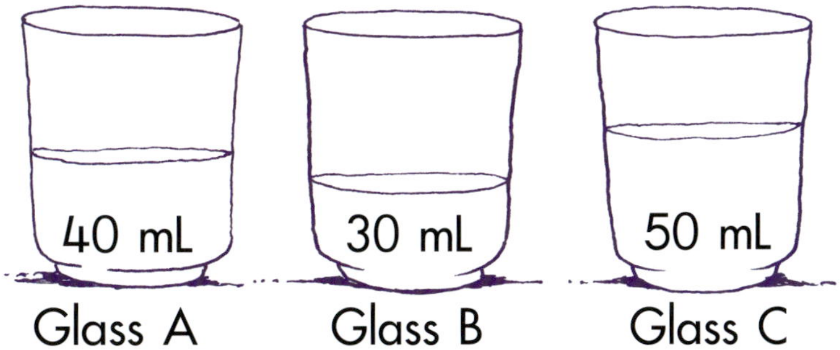

What must Ruby do to make them equal?

Extension

If Ruby wanted to pour all the juice into just 2 equal glasses, how much would be in each glass?

Strategy hints!

1. Look for the important words in the question.
5. Use a drawing.
9. Think logically.

ISBN 978 1 4202 9393 7

SOMETHING DIFFERENT

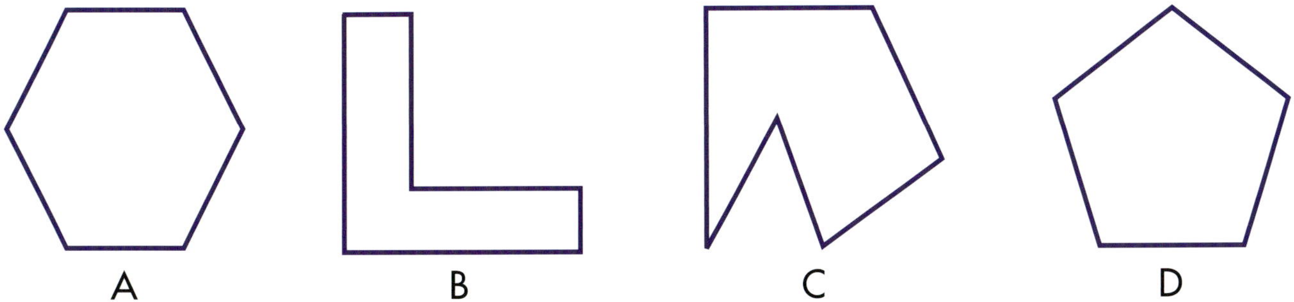

Which shape is not like the others?

Extension

Make up a problem like this one.

See if a classmate can work it out.

Strategy hints!

1 Look for the important words in the question.

5 Use a drawing.

9 Think logically.

ISBN 978 1 4202 9393 7

CUT IT OUT

Jacob folds a piece of paper in half and cuts out a piece.
He then unfolds it.

What will it look like?

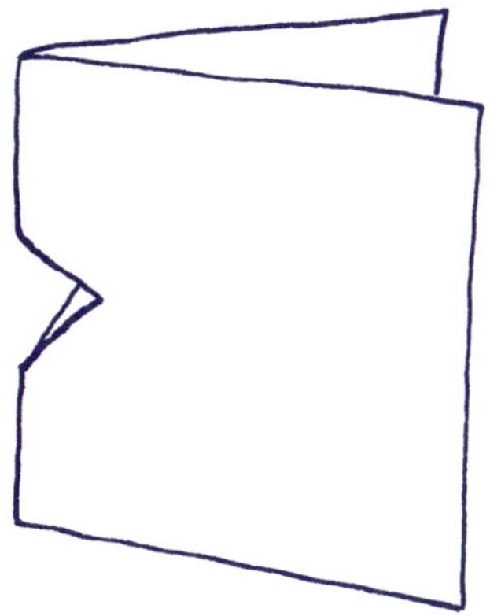

Extension

Sally folds a piece of paper in half and cuts out a piece.
She then unfolds it.
What will it look like?

Strategy hints!

1. Look for the important words in the question.
5. Use a drawing.
8. Make a model.

ISBN 978 1 4202 9393 7

WHICH HOLDS MOST?

Jordan looks at 3 vases:

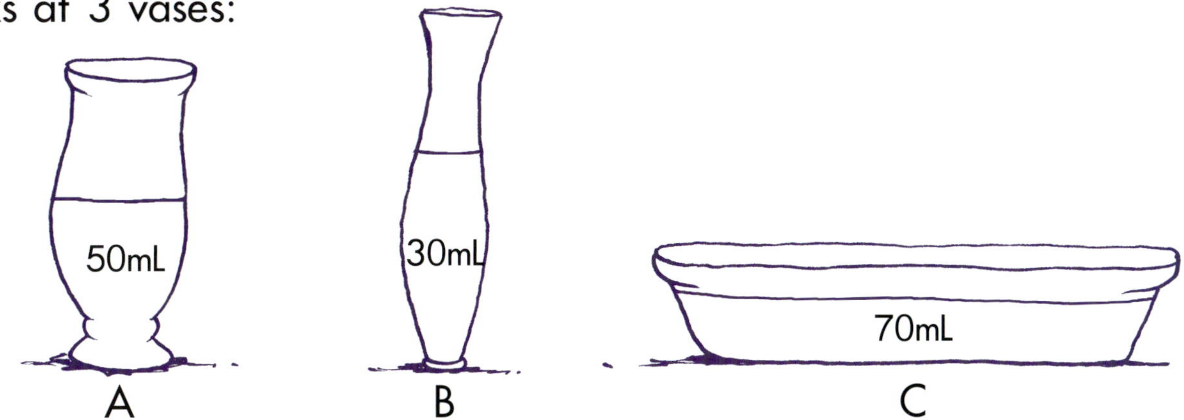

Put them in order from the least amount of water to the most amount of water.

Extension

If all 3 vases were full to the top, which would hold the most amount of water?

Strategy hints!

1 Look for the important words in the question.

5 Use a drawing.

9 Think logically.

ISBN 978 1 4202 9393 7

LIGHT BAR TIME

Georgia looks at her digital clock.
It shows 1 o'clock.

Georgia sees that this time uses 14 light bars.

When Georgia comes home it is an o'clock time that uses 16 light bars.
What time could it be?

Extension

There is a time that uses only 6 light bars on a digital clock. What time is this?

Strategy hints!

1 Look for the important words in the question.

5 Use a drawing.

9 Think logically.

ISBN 978 1 4202 9393 7

SHAPE LOGIC

Draw a straight line.
Now, draw a cross.
Now, draw a triangle.

What might you draw next?

Extension

a) How many corners will the 5th and 6th shapes have?
b) How many corners will the 9th shape have?

Strategy hints!

1 Look for the important words in the question.

9 Think logically.

ISBN 978 1 4202 9393 7

A SHAPELY PUZZLE

∩	⊃	∪	⊂	∩	?
1	2	3	4	5	6

Which of these 4 shapes will come next in the pattern?

⊃	∪	∩	⊂
A	B	C	D

Extension

a) What shape will come in 10th place?

b) What shape will come in 15th place?

Strategy hints!

1. Look for the important words in the question.
2. Look for a pattern.
9. Think logically.

ISBN 978 1 4202 9393 7

STATISTICS AND PROBABILITY

HAVE A SPIN

Isabella looks at 4 spinners.

She wants to spin red.

Which spinner will give her the best chance of spinning red?

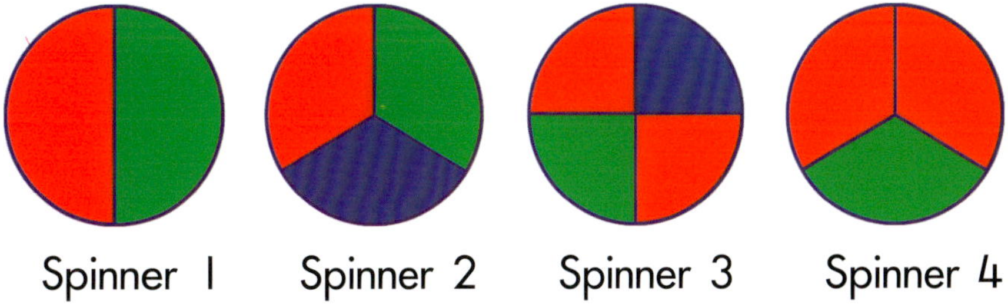

Extension

There are 2 spinners that have the same chance of spinning red. Which are they?

Strategy hints!

1 Look for the important words in the question.

5 Use a drawing.

9 Think logically.

ISBN 978 1 4202 9393 7

SPORTS VOTES

The 24 students in Year 1 voted for their favourite sports.
The results were recorded in a table.

Sport	Votes
swimming	3
football	11
netball	6
soccer	?

a) How many students voted for soccer?

b) List the sports in order from most popular to least popular.

Extension

Make up a problem like this one.
See if a classmate can work it out.

Strategy hints!

1 Look for the important words in the question.

4 Use a table or a chart.

9 Think logically.

ISBN 978 1 4202 9393 7

LUCKY DIP

Tom puts his hand into a bag. He can't see what is inside.
Inside are 10 marbles.
3 are red, 5 are green and 2 are yellow.

What is the chance of taking out a red marble?

Is it:

- Certain?
- Likely?
- Possible?
- Impossible?

Extension

List the 3 colours in order of least likely to most likely.

Strategy hints!

1. Look for the important words in the question.
5. Use a drawing.
9. Think logically.

ISBN 978 1 4202 9393 7

CAR COLOURS

Here are the colours of 3 teachers' cars.

	Green	Black	White
Mr Green		✓	
Mr White			✓
Mr Black	✓		

a) Which teacher has a car that is the same colour as his name?

b) All the teachers want to drive cars that are the same colour as their name. Who will have to drive Mr Green's car?

Extension

Three children each own a pet. The pets are a fish, a bird and a dog.
Daisy's pet has more legs than Amy's pet. Brad's pet has no legs at all.
Who owns which pet?

Strategy hints!

1 Look for the important words in the question.
4 Use a table or a chart.
9 Think logically.

ISBN 978 1 4202 9393 7

COIN TOSS

A coin has heads on one side and tails on the other.
Haylie tosses the coin 6 times.
It comes up heads, tails, heads, tails, heads, tails.

Does tails have the best chance of being tossed next?

Extension

After 2 more tosses, what number of tails and heads are possible?

Strategy hints!

1 Look for the important words in the question.

9 Think logically.

ISBN 978 1 4202 9393 7

WEEKEND FAVOURITES

Ollie and Sophie made a graph of the time they spend doing things on the weekend.

Each picture stands for 1 hour.

Do Ollie and Sophie spend more time watching TV or playing sport on the weekend?

	TV	Sport
Ollie		
Sophie		

Extension

Ollie played sport for an hour longer on Saturday than on Sunday.
How many minutes did Ollie play sport on Sunday?

Strategy hints!

1 Look for the important words in the question.

4 Use a table or a chart.

9 Think logically.

ISBN 978 1 4202 9393 7

TAKE A CARD

The teacher has 5 cards numbered 1, 2, 3, 4 and 5.
She turns them face down and mixes them up.
She points to the top card and says, "This card is an even number."

Is it best to say:

- "Yes, I think so too."?
- "No, I don't think so."?
- "It can't possibly be even."?

Extension

Make up a question that should be answered, "That's impossible."

Strategy hints!

1 Look for the important words in the question.
5 Use a drawing.
9 Think logically.

ISBN 978 1 4202 9393 7

PETS AT HOME

In year 1, 7 students were asked about the pet they had at home.
The results were recorded in a table.

Name	Pet
Andrew	fish
Beth	cat
Charlie	dog
Ollie	lizard
Emma	dog
Franz	cat
Rachael	fish

a) What is the total number of legs of the pets in the table?

b) Are there more warm-blooded pets, or more cold-blooded pets?

Extension

Harry was then asked about his pet at home. When his pet was added to the table, there was an equal number of each animal. What pet does Harry have?

Strategy hints!

1 Look for the important words in the question.

4 Use a table or a chart.

9 Think logically.

ISBN 978 1 4202 9393 7

SPIN A PRIZE

If you spin the spinner, which numbers will come up:

a) Most often?

b) Second most often?

c) Least often?

Extension

If you spin the spinner 18 times, how many times do you think it should land on 1?

Strategy hints!

1 Look for the important words in the question.

5 Use a drawing.

9 Think logically.

ISBN 978 1 4202 9393 7

10 BOYS AND 10 GIRLS

My Year 1 class has 10 boys and 10 girls in it.
The teacher, Mrs Picker, puts the names of the students into a hat.
She then takes out 3 names.
The names are all boys.

Does the next name she takes out have the best chance of being:

- a boy?
- a girl?
- both boys and girls have the same chance?

Extension

My name came out 4th. Am I most likely to be a boy or a girl?

Strategy hints!

1 Look for the important words in the question.

9 Think logically.

ISBN 978 1 4202 9393 7

ANSWERS

Number and Algebra

Answers 1

1. **Code cracker**: Tree
(Hint: Each number is the letter order of the alphabet.)
Extension: Answers will vary.

2. **Letters and numbers**: **a)** CAT = 3 + 1 + 20 = 24;
b) ANT = 1 + 14 + 20 = 35;
c) FROG = 6 + 18 + 15 + 7 = 46
(Hint: The letters are worth their place in the alphabet.)
Extension: Answers will vary.

3. **Funny pattern**: R, P, L
(Hint: It is the alphabet backwards, missing every second letter.)
Extension: F, D, B

4. **Symbol shifter**: **a)** 14; **b)** [*] means to add the numbers together and then add on 1 more.
Extension: Answers will vary.

5. **Find the symbol**: **a)** 5; **b)** [*] means to take away the 2nd number and then take away another 2.
Extension: Answers will vary.

6. **Crazy calculator**: 8
(Hint: The 2 digits are added together, 2 + 6 = 8.)
Extension: Answers will vary.

7. **Dizzy digits**: 3
(Hint: The 2nd digit is being taken away from the 1st, 7 – 4 = 3.)
Extension: Answers will vary.

8. **Boxed in**: 2 answers: 4 + 6 – 3 + 2 = 9
or 4 + 2 – 3 + 6 = 9
Extension: 2 answers: 5 + 7 – 4 – 3 = 5
or 5 + 7 – 3 – 4 = 5

9. **Inside the box**: 2 answers: 10 – 5 – 4 = 2 – 1
or 10 – 4 – 5 = 2 – 1
(Hint: Start with the biggest number.)
Extension: 2 answers: 10 + 3 – 11 = 14 – 12
or 3 + 10 – 11 = 14 – 12

ISBN 978 1 4202 9393 7

10. Boxed up: 2 answers
1: 10 – 6 + 3 = 8 – 1
2: 10 – 6 + 1 = 8 – 3
Extension: 4 answers
1: 7 – 3 – 2 = 10 – 8
2: 7 – 2 – 3 = 10 – 8
3: 8 – 3 – 2 = 10 – 7
4: 8 – 2 – 3 = 10 – 7

11. Light bar logic: 5 and 6
Extension: 8

12. Light it up: 11
Extension: 2, 3 and 5

13. Light bar look: 14, 41 and 71
Extension: 111
(Hint: 1 only uses 2 light bars so you can get a big answer.)

14. Bears and rabbits: $9
Extension: **a)** $24; **b)** $54
(Hint: Find the price of the bear first by taking away.)

15. Shirts and shorts: $12
Extension: **a)** $16; **b)** $52
(Hint: Find the answer by taking away.)

16. Cars and dolls: $6
Extension: **a)** $28; **b)** $42
(Hint: Find the answer by taking away.)

17. Books and bookmarks: $9
(Hint: Start with the book and the bookmark costing the same and then move the prices apart.)
Extension: Answers will vary.

ISBN 978 1 4202 9393 7

18. 20 cents:

1: 20c
2: 10c + 10c
3: 10c + 5c + 5c
4: 5c + 5c + 5c + 5c

Extension: **a)** 4 ways

1: 20c + 5c
2: 10c + 10c + 5c
3: 10c + 5c + 5c + 5c
4: 5c + 5c + 5c + 5c + 5c

b) 13 ways

1: 50c
2: 20c + 20 + 10c
3: 20c + 10c + 10c + 10c
4: 20c + 20c + 5c + 5c
5: 20c + 10c + 10c + 5c + 5c
6: 20c + 10c + 5c + 5c + 5c + 5c
7: 20c + 5c + 5c + 5c + 5c + 5c + 5c + 5c + 5c
8: 10c + 10c + 10c + 10c + 10c
9: 10c + 10c + 10c + 10c + 5c + 5c
10: 10c + 10c + 10c + 5c + 5c + 5c + 5c
11: 10c + 10c + 5c + 5c + 5c + 5c + 5c + 5c
12: 10c + 5c + 5c + 5c + 5c + 5c + 5c + 5c + 5c
13: 5c + 5c + 5c + 5c + 5c + 5c + 5c + 5c + 5c + 5c

19. What number am I?: 90
(Hint: 9 + 0 = 9, which is an odd number.)
Extension: Answers will vary.

20. Find my number: 14, 23, 32, 41, 50
(Hint: 14 helps with 41 and 23 helps with 32.)
Extension: Answers will vary.

21. Who am I?: 3, 7 or 9
(Hint: Type all of the numbers from 1 to 9 into the calculator to check this answer.)
Extension: Answers will vary.

22. Name my number: 41, 43, 45, 47, 49
(Hint: The 4 must be in the 10s place.)
Extension: 34, 40, 42, 44, 46, 48

23. Guess the digits: 50
Extension: 70
(Hint: The number has to end in a zero.)

ISBN 978 1 4202 9393 7

24. Equal animals: 4
(Hint: These animals are on our coins.)
Extension: **a)** 5; **b)** 5

25. Line up please: 14 students
(Hint: Sara needs to be counted as well.)
Extension: Answers will vary.

26. Line logic: 10 students
(Hint: 10 will be in front of Zac and 10 will be behind him.)
Extension: Answers will vary.

27. Fair share: 3 stickers
Extension: No, it won't work unless the numbers are both odd or both even.

28. Sticker share: 4 stickers
Extension: No, it won't work unless the number of stickers is in the 3s counting pattern.

29. How old? 4 years old
(Hint: We know Jack is 5.)
Extension: Answers will vary.

30. Age to age: Owen, Ramesh, Claire
Extension: Owen, Ramesh, Claire, Kaitlin, Joey
(Hint: The age of the children can be guessed from the sentences.)

31. How many numbers? 33, 35, 38, 53, 55, 58, 83, 85, 88
(Hint: It is easiest to list them from smallest to biggest.)
Extension: 11, 17, 18, 71, 77, 78, 81, 87, 88. There will always be 9 answers as long as the 3 numbers are different.

32. Numbers up: 22, 27, 72, 77
Extension: 44, 48, 84, 88. There will always be 4 answers as long as 2 of the 3 numbers are the same.

33. Target time: 3 + 5 + 7 or 5 + 5 + 5
Extension: 14 (7 + 7)
(Hint: He can score the same total more than once.)

34. Aim the arrow: 10 + 10 + 7
Extension: 3 + 3 + 7
(Hint: 3 + 3 + 7 = 13)

ISBN 978 1 4202 9393 7

35. **Funny numbers**: 12, 24, 36, 48
Extension: 21, 42, 63, 84

36. **Unique numbers**: 18, 27, 36, 45, 54, 63, 72, 81, 90
Extension: 17, 26, 35, 44, 53, 62, 71, 80
(Hint: One answer can often help to get another.)

37. **All the twos**: 13 times: 2, 12, 20, 21, 22, 23, 24, 25, 26, 27, 28, 29
Extension: 13 times: 35, 45, 50, 51, 52, 53, 54, 55, 56, 57, 58, 59
(Hint: In 22 and 55 there are two 2s and two 5s.)

38. **All the numbers**: 31 digits
(Hint: 1 for every 1-digit number and 2 for every 2-digit number.)
Extension: 20 digits

39. **Where did he start?**: $22
(Hint: Start at the end and then move to the start of the question.)
Extension: Answers will vary.

40. **Money share**: $6
(Hint: Start at the end and then move to the start of the question.)
Extension: $8

41. **How much money?**: $16
(Hint: Start at the end and then move to the start of the question: $3 + $3 + $10 = $16.)
Extension: Answers will vary.

42. **Column craft**: A = numbers in the 5s counting pattern, end in 5 or 0
B = numbers in the 2s counting pattern, end in 2, 4, 6, 8 or 0
C= numbers in the 10s counting pattern, end in 0
Extension: **a)** 90 is in the 2, 5 and 10 patterns;
b) 9 numbers: 10, 20, 30, 40, 50, 60, 70, 80, 90

43. **Crazy columns**: 92 and 93 should be switched.
(Hint: Column A is odd numbers and column B is even numbers.)
Extension: A: 997, 999; B: 996, 998

ISBN 978 1 4202 9393 7

44. Odd one out: Answers will vary. Answers may include:
7, only odd number or only single digit number
54, digits differ by 1
64, highest number on the list
Extension: Answers will vary. Answers may include:
22, two digits the same
107, only 3-digit number
40, only number in the 10s counting pattern
56, only number with one odd and one even digit.

45. 40 cents: 10c + 5c + 5c + 5c + 5c + 5c + 5c
Extension: 3 ways
1: 20c + 20c
2: 20c + 10c + 10c
3: 10c + 10c + 10c + 10c

46. Magic square:

8	1	6
3	5	7
4	9	2

Extension: There are many answers that work, but will all have 5 in the centre.

47. Backwards and forwards: What is added is taken away to equal zero.
Extension: What is added is taken away to equal zero.

48. Letterboxes: 12 houses
(Hint: Skip count in 2s starting with 1.)
Extension: 7 or 8 houses. 10, 12, 14, 16, 18, 20, 22 and 24

49. Street numbers: 7 houses
(Hint: On Grandma's side are house numbers 1, 3, 5, 7, 9, 11 and 13.)
Extension: Number 11

50. Need a lift?: 2 levels
Extension: Answers will vary.

51. Lift me higher: 5 times
(Hint: When you go up 1 level and then down 2 levels it is like dropping 1 level.)
Extension: 25 times

52. Consecutive challenge: 8 and 9
(Hint: Try at about halfway.)
Extension: **a)** 15 and 16; **b)** 26 and 27

ISBN 978 1 4202 9393 7

53. Number neighbours: 5, 6 and 7
(Hint: Split the number into 3 parts.)
Extension: **a)** 9, 10 and 11; **b)** 14, 15 and 16

54. Leg work: **a)** 2 dogs; **b)** 1 bird
(Hint: 4 + 4 + 2 = 10)
Extension: **a)** 2 ladybirds;
b) 1 spider (6 + 6 + 8 = 20)

55. Paws and claws: **a)** 2 cats; **b)** 3 chickens
(Hint: 2 + 2 + 2 + 4 + 4 = 14)
Extension: Answers will vary.

56. Birthday bonanza: **a)** The money is doubling each year; **b)** She gets $16.
(Hint: 1, 2, 4, 8, 16, 32)
Extension: **a)** 6 years old; **b)** 8 years old

57. Number cruncher: 4 (four)
Extension: 2 (two) and 5 (five)

58. Which column?: **a)** B; **b)** D; **c)** C; **d)** A
(Hint: Look for a pattern.)
Extension: B, D

59. Number columns: **a)** A; **b)** C; **c)** B; **d)** D; **e)** A
(Hint: Look for a pattern.)
Extension: D

60. Follow the symbols: 16
(Hint: 10 − 1 + 3 + 3 + 2 − 1 = 16)
Extension: 15 (15 + 3 − 1 − 1 + 2 + 2 = 20. Start at 20 and work backwards.)

61. Missing number: 9
(Hint: Find the gap between 11 and 20 by taking away.)
Extension: 9

62. Two boxes the same: **a)** 6 + 6; **b)** 4 + 4 + 4;
c) 3 + 3 + 3 + 3
(Hint: Find half of 12.)
Extension: 12 answers

0+ 12	7 + 5
1 + 11	8 + 4
2 + 10	9 + 3
3 + 9	10 + 2
4 + 8	11 + 1
5 + 7	12 + 0

ISBN 978 1 4202 9393 7

63. Different ages: 9
(Hint: Make Otto as young as he could possibly be.)
Extension: 18 years old

64. Find the ages: 6, 8, 10
(Hint: Below 6 the difference can't equal 5 years.)
Extension: Kim's age must be odd because an even number taken away from an even number can't be odd.

65. What if?: 6 (4 + 5 – 3 = 6)
(Hint: Add 2 to each number.)
Extension: Answers will vary.

66. All about Beth: 9
(Hint: Do the opposite of what Beth says. Beth must be younger than 10 and her age must be an odd number.)
Extension: Answers will vary.

67. 50 cents: 20c + 20c + 5c + 5c
or 20c + 10c + 10c + 10c
(Hint: See if any other answer will work.)
Extension: $8 ($2 + $2 + $2 + $2)

68. Different numbers: 48 + 52
(Hint: Start with 50 and 50 and then move apart.)
Extension: 99 + 1

69. Grandma and Grandad: 91
(Hint: 91 is as close to 100 – 10 as possible.)
Extension: 6 (94 – 88 = 6)

70. Shopping: **a)** $30;
b) $2 + $2 + $2 + $2 + $2 + $1
(Hint: $11 + $9 + $10 = $30)
Extension: Answers will vary.

71. Shoe size: 9 (nine)
(Hint: No other numbers in the 3s counting pattern have 4 letters in their number name.)
Extension: Answers will vary.

72. Numbers line up: 15
(Hint: The numbers must be 4, 5 and 6.)
Extension: 6, 7 and 8

73. Bon and Ben: 1, 2, 3, 4 or 5
(Hint: Ben must be younger than 6.)
Extension: 22 years

ISBN 978 1 4202 9393 7

Number and Algebra

Answers 9

74. Egyptian numerals: 23
(Hint: The order of the symbols did not matter. 10 + 2 + 10 + 1 = 23)
Extension: Answers will vary.

75. Alien numerals: 14
(Hint: 2 + 5 + 7)
Extension: Answers will vary.

76. 2-digit numbers: 87
(Hint: 97 – 10)
Extension: 98 – 11 = 87. The answers are the same.

77. Different digits: 8 answers
1: 12 and 21
2: 23 and 32
3: 34 and 43
4: 45 and 54
5: 56 and 65
6: 67 and 76
7: 78 and 87
8: 89 and 98
(Hint: The digits used must be very close.)
Extension: 19 and 91

78. Toy sale: 2 planes, 1 bear, 1 boat
Extension: 1 plane, 3 boats

79. Main Town: 12 kilometres
(Hint: 12 is half of 24)
Extension: From Ambley to Main Town is 12 km. From Main Town to Clarke is 6 km. From Clarke to Gotley is 6 km.

80. Coloured pencils: 9
(Hint: 40 – 10 – 5 – 16 = 9)
Extension: 5, 6, 7, or 8

81. Counting in threes: No
(Hint: 2, 5, 8, 11, 14, 17, 20, 23, 26, 29, 32)
Extension: 59

82. Big Town: 16
(Hint: 10 + 8 – 2 = 16)
Extension: Answers will vary.

83. Race place: 21 runners
(Hint: 18 + 3 = 21)
Extension: **a)** 4 runners; **b)** 16 runners

ISBN 978 1 4202 9393 7

84. Up to 20: 6
(Hint: 1 + 2 + 3 + 4 + 5 + 6 = 21)
Extension: **a)** 8 (1 + 2 + 3 + 4 + 5 + 6 + 7 + 8);
b) 34 (7 + 8 + 9 + 10 = 34)

85. 20 plus: 8
(Hint: 5 + 6 = 11 leaving 9 to make 20)
Extension: 17

86. Even Steven: 20
(Hint: This is a half of 40.)
Extension: 20

87. Box puzzle: 3 ways
1: 31 + 4 + 6 or 31 + 6 + 4
2: 34 + 1 + 6 or 34 + 6 + 1
3: 36 + 1 + 4 or 36 + 4 + 1
(Hint: The 3 must be in the 10s place.)
Extension: Answers will vary.

88. Many ways: 8 ways
1: 10 + 1 + 9
2: 10 + 2 + 8
3: 10 + 8 + 2
4: 10 + 3 + 7
5: 10 + 7 + 3
6: 10 + 6 + 4
7: 10 + 4 + 6
8: 10 + 5 + 5
Extension: Answers will vary.

89. Number thinking: 50
(Hint: It must end in a zero.)
Extension: 71, 73, 79

90. Adding up: **a)** 8 + 5; **b)** 5 + 14
(Hint: Start with 2 very close numbers, like 6 and 7, then move them further apart.)
Extension: Answers will vary.

91. 20 puzzle: 4 ways
1: 4 + 16
2: 6 + 14
3: 8 + 12
4: 10 + 10
(Hint: The order of the 2 numbers does not matter.)
Extension: 15 + 15

ISBN 978 1 4202 9393 7

92. Calculator mix-up: 8
(Hint: 6 + 4 = 10 and 6 – 4 = 2. 10 – 2 = 8.)
Extension: 10 (6 + 4 + 5 = 15 and 6 + 4 – 5 = 10. 15 – 10 = 5)

93. Stamp sale: $1
(Hint: $13 – $10 – $2 = $1)
Extension: 6 stamps

94. Missing number: 2
(Hint: Make groups of 10. 5 + 5 = 10, 6 + 4 = 10, 8 + 2 = 10)
Extension: 1 and 8 (9 + 1 = 10, 2 + 8 = 10)

95. Close to 35: 33
(Hint: 33 is only 2 away from 35.)
Extension: **a)** Yes; **b)** No, because all of the numbers end in either 3 or 8.

96. Add to itself: **a)** 5; **b)** 13
(Hint: Change adding to itself to half the number to find the answer.)
Extension: **a)** 4; **b)** 8

97. Double up: **a)** 7 or 8; **b)** 12 or 13
(Hint: Halve 13 which is 6 or 7, and halve 25 which is 12 or 13.)
Extension: **a)** 15 or 16; **b)** 50 or 51

98. Open book: Pages 10 and 11
(Hint: The pages must be numbers that follow on from each other.)
Extension: No. One page must be even and one page odd so they can't add up to an even number.

99. Halfway through: **a)** 60 pages; **b)** 104 pages
(Hint: Double the page you are on.)
Extension: 52 pages

100. 2 books high: 2 cm and 4 cm
(Hint: 2 is half of 4.)
Extension: 5 cm and 10 cm

ISBN 978 1 4202 9393 7

Measurement and Geometry

Answers 12

1. **Pencils and rulers**: 4 rulers
   (Hint: Every 1 ruler will equal 3 pencils.)
   Extension: 36 pencils
2. **Paints and paintbrushes**: 4 brushes
   (Hint: The 4th brush will go past the 7th tube of paint.)
   Extension: 9 erasers
3. **Blocks for sale**: $14
   (Hint: 7 lots of $2)
   Extension: **a)** 13 blocks; **b)** 20 blocks
4. **Insect lengths**: Flea, ant, bee, wasp
   (Hint: Try using a drawing to match the facts.)
   Extension: Answers will vary.
5. **All the triangles**: 5 triangles
   (Hint: The whole picture is a triangle too.)
   Extension: 5 triangles
6. **All the squares**: 8 squares
   (Hint: 2 of the squares overlap.)
   Extension: 11 squares
7. **Training**: 5 days: 3rd, 14th, 17th, 28th, 31st
   Extension: October
8. **Time pattern**: J, A, S
   (Hint: The letters stand for months of the year.)
   Extension: 14th
9. **V shape**: B and D
   (Hint: The V shape in picture D has been turned.)
   Extension: D
10. **Missing part**: 5 blocks
    (Hint: The shape should be 5 long and 4 high.)
    Extension: 10 blocks. The square will be 5 long and 5 high.
11. **Paper cut**: Square

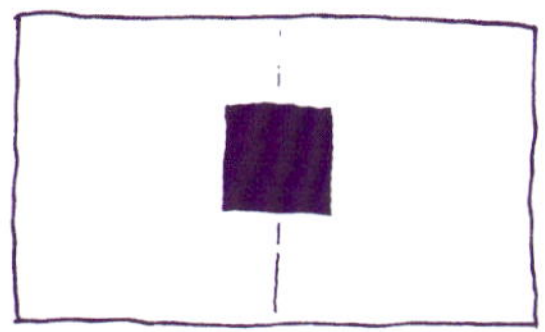

(Hint: Practice with a real piece of paper and scissors.)
Extension: Answers will vary.

ISBN 978 1 4202 9393 7

12. **Corners, edges, faces**: Edges
(Hint: There are 12 edges, 6 faces and 8 corners.)
Extension: 12 edges, 6 faces and 8 corners. The same as the original shape.

13. **Digital challenge**: 13
(Hint: 2 + 5 + 6)
Extension: 16 (5 + 5 + 6)

14. **Handy hands**: 3:30
(Hint: The big hand is the minutes and the little hand is the hours.)
Extension: 5:00

15. **Arrowheads**: **a)** ↑ **b)** ↓
(Hint: The pattern is up, right, down left.)
Extension: **a)** ↑ **b)** ←

16. **Netball times**: 1 hour 30 minutes
(Hint: 10 o'clock to 11 o'clock = 1 hour and then add on 30 minutes.)
Extension: 30 minutes

17. **Karate training**: 25th and 30th
(Hint: Weng trains on days in the 5s counting pattern.)
Extension: February has only 28 or 29 days.

18. **Not like the others**: A
(Hint: A is the only shape with a curved side.)
Extension: Answers will vary.

19. **Equal glasses**: Ruby should pour 10 mL from glass C into glass B.
Extension: 60 mL each

20. **Something different**: D
(Hint: The other 3 shapes use 6 lines.)
Extension: Answers will vary.

21. **Cut it out**: Diamond with equal sides

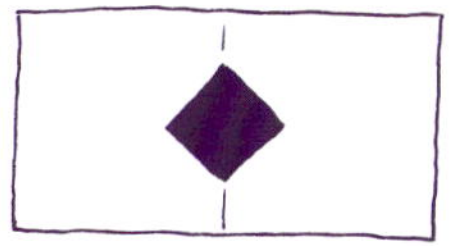

Extension: Hexagon

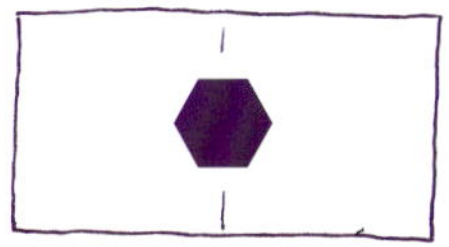

ISBN 978 1 4202 9393 7

22. Which holds most?: B, A, C
(Hint: Vase C is the shortest but the number of mL is the biggest.)
Extension: Vase C

23. Light bar time: 4:00 or 7:00 or 11:00
(Hint: 4 + 6 + 6)
Extension: 1:11

24. Shape logic: A 4-sided figure such as a square or rectangle
(Hint: You are using 1 more line each time.)
Extension: **a)** 5 and 6 corners; **b)** 9 corners

25. A shapely puzzle: A
(Hint: The shapes are turning a quarter turn each time.)
Extension: **a)** A; **b)** B

ISBN 978 1 4202 9393 7

Statistics and Probability

Answers 15

1. **Have a spin**: Spinner 4
(Hint: It has the biggest part showing red.)
Extension: Spinners 1 and 3

2. **Sports votes**: **a)** 4; **b)** Football, netball, soccer, swimming
(Hint: 11 + 6 + 3 + 4 = 24)
Extension: Answers will vary.

3. **Lucky dip**: Possible
(Hint: There are more marbles that are not red.)
Extension: Yellow, red, green

4. **Car colours**: **a)** Mr White; **b)** Mr Black
(Hint: Mr White + white car)
Extension: Daisy owns the dog, Amy owns the bird and Brad owns the fish.

5. **Coin toss**: Heads and tails have the same chance.
(Hint: For each toss, heads and tails are 50/50.)
Extension: 3 heads + 5 tails or 4 heads + 4 tails or 5 heads + 3 tails

6. **Weekend favourites**: TV
(Hint: TV was 7 hours. Sport was 6 hours and 30 minutes.)
Extension: 60 minutes

7. **Take a card**: No, I don't think so.
(Hint: There is a bigger chance that the card will be odd.)
Extension: Answers will vary.

8. **Pets at home**: **a)** 20 (5 groups of 4);
b) More are warm-blooded.
(Hint: The dogs and cats are warm-blooded.)
Extension: Lizard

9. **Spin a prize**: **a)** 3; **b)** 2; **c)** 1
Extension: 3 times

10. **10 boys and 10 girls**: A girl
(Hint: There are 10 girls and only 7 boys' names left in the hat.)
Extension: A girl

ISBN 978 1 4202 9393 7